SKY

LIGHT

By Raushan Mahdee

To my family and friends

Table of Contents

Printed in the United States

ISBN 13: 978-0692089354
ISBN 10: 0692089357

Illustrations by

Raushan Mahdee

-Forbidden Fruit

<u>Late Bloomer</u>

A storm brews

The wind growls and howls

Fire burns

Ashes fill the urn

Light cannot curve

But it follows me around every turn

Skylight

01 Oct 2003

"You're not crazy, you're a dreamer. A true believer."

Raushan Mahdee

Dreams

When dreamers dream, do they dream of dreams?

Or do they dream of love, maybe of doves or the heavens above?

Do they dream of flying or dream of dying?

Perhaps they dream of lying on clouds that cover the earth

What is a dream but of things that we create while we are asleep?

Which dreams are worth fighting for?

And why does the loss of dreams cause us to weep?

Let your dreams take you places

And let it be a great escape

Because dreams are wonderful things

Doesn't matter if you are asleep or awake

Skylight

02 Dec 2017

"What is your definition of normal?"

Raushan Mahdee

Introvert

We don't understand you

So that gives us the right to judge you

Obscure view of individuality

Blindsides our rationality

We want to see your personality

But in reality

That frightens the shit out of our mentality

Even though we shout and pout about originality

Smile for awhile

Life isn't that bad

Why do you hang your head so low?

Why do you seem so sad?

We can tell you how to live

Because we got our lives together

So, that makes us better

We're always happy

We want the same for you

Because you seem so crabby

We can change your whole view

Skylight

Conform to society

But also show some variety

Just be normal

Informal

Information

For your inconsideration

Makes this generation

An abomination

But you're a coward

So it makes sense for you to avoid this conversation

Raushan Mahdee

<u>Rain Water</u>

I have

    focus and determination

        And I've been patiently waiting for

                    inspiration

Hoping and wishing

        For a fantastic opportunity to fall into my lap

Procrastination is a cancer

I'm consistently content with being completely complacent

        Easily distracted

With social media interactions

        Losing traction

    I feel like my grip on reality is loose

        My mind is held hostage by the news

I'm such a critic, I can hardly contain my own opinions

Judging others so harshly and not accomplishing anything

Skylight

The world is fake and that's my take

People screaming woke

But still won't wake at the sound of the alarms that call

them to start their day

Stop dreaming because it seems that your dreams are

taking you far away from reality

My mind is blank, living in society's neutrality

Raushan Mahdee

<u>**03**</u> Dec 2005

"The world is cruel and depression is real. The life we live is truly unfair."

Skylight

Misery part 1

Mistaking my own faith

Maybe to maintain my own fate

Drinking poison to battle loneliness

Death rattles my fragile bones

Frozen in time and abandoned at home

Oceans bubbling, monsters rising from the sea foam

Cold sweats

Keep me up at night

Bright white lights burning my eyes

I'm begging the Lord to give me the strength to fight

Misplaced

Because of my race

Feeling like I was born a mistake

Lately I'm just trying to suffocate the hate

State of depression heavy on my mind

Treated unfairly, even by my own kind

Choking on rain water trying to stay afloat

Pressure building up and I have a knife at my throat

Never belonged anywhere, never had a choice

Writing stories trying to figure out my own voice

17

Raushan Mahdee

Self-esteem exhausting of steam

As a young teen

I wish living in Misery was only a dream

Careless life of sin

Locked emotions inside of a den

Misery got me feeling less than human because of my skin...

Skylight Part One

Red ink flowing from my veins

Staining the page that I'm writing in

With my pen

Feelings of devastation

Living my life, the way it is

Crossing the line

Only to find

I was wrong about everything

The things I lost

I regret losing

The people I chose

I regret choosing

Eyes rolled back into my skull

I'm lying on the ice cold

Hardwood floor

My body is shaking

I think this poison is taking control

Clashing harsh waves

Destroying deserted dark caves

A mind once hopeful now bleeding hopelessly

How can darkness fill a heart so quickly, that was once full of glee?

Skylight

"Betrayal can be a real son of a bitch"

Raushan Mahdee

Friends

Lost identity and lost contact

Trying to explain the ambiguity and digress

Mid-sentence

Uneasy to impress

But easily stressed

Wearing a mask to cover the insecurity

But show imaginary happiness

I tried to keep in contact with y'all

But you all weren't returning my phone calls

So called friends to the end but only play pretend

Secretly hating me and don't want me to win

Dust in the wind

Demons lies being whispered in my ears

Gotta rely on my mind. So far, it's still clear

Until it turns against me too

What am I to do?

I could never be liked for myself so I guess I lose

All for likes

You don't really care about anyone else

Only thing that you're concerned with is only yourself

Taking selfies by the seashore with expensive shellfish

Just admit it you're fucking selfish

It's just complete non-sense

Fueling your foolish ego

In the midst to discover true happiness

But you can't understand absolute bliss

Has disappeared in the abyss

Fearing the judgement of your peers

Eyes piercing through your soul

Making you paranoid with some kind of guilt

Self-doubted, mind clouded in darkness

Can you hearken to your heart crying for help?

Thinking that nobody loves you

Thinking that no one cares for you

Thinking that no one is thinking of you

You don't even have a clue

Just ignorant to the environment that surrounds you

Trying to impress strangers

Pressured into sharing things

Because you feel like you have something to prove

But you forget the people nearest to you

LOVE you for YOU

LOST

Back on Doris drive when I felt alive

Last experience of innocence before I became corrupt

Abrupt way of thinking

Thinking that I could be somebody

Vitalizing my visual sensibility to become number one

But I never won

Realization of never being accepted

I wish I could go back to the days of my adolescence

Fast forward to the latter half of nineteen ninety-nine

The millennium birthed the illusion of independence

And produced sensitive bastards that have no influences

Embarrassed to be themselves

Only carbon copies of each other

Rinse. Dry. Repeat.

Half Complete

Competitive but can't compete

A travesty

Of an absolute catastrophe

Awarded participation trophies

To encourage them

Unhinge the staples of the mind

Privileged mindsets have chosen their future in advance

Never had a chance

They should live humble because life can be over in a glance

Skylight

<u>05</u> Sep 2014

"It's all about perspectives, never forget that."

Raushan Mahdee

Skylight Part Two

All I wanted to do was die

I was regretting my plans

Once I heard my mother cry

But, it's too late

Once my eyes were closed

I was asking God, why?

Why me O' Lord?

Are you doing this because you're bored?

What is my lesson?

Every time I tried to achieve happiness

Its stripped away from me with no hesitation

No explanation

Skylight

I'm angry, frustrated

And hell bent on retaliation

What is my worth?

Why was I put here on this earth?

Running around in circles trying to escape my own depression

My mind is bursting at the seams with so many questions

That will never be answered

I'm tired and infuriated

I tried to inspire

But hopes and dreams ended up expired

I know killing myself might be considered wrong

But I feel like you will only love me as soon as I'm gone

06 Nov ????

"I didn't know how much I missed her, until I saw her. I didn't know how much I loved her, until I looked into her eyes. I didn't know how much I needed her, until I held her in my arms. I didn't know a woman like **HER** could ever exist."

Skylight

HER

Stumbling rumbling cadence of a heart beat

Stampede

Tumbling crumbling hiding the secrets we keep

Shhh don't speak

Pulled the floor boards from underneath my feet

A promise I want to keep before I'm six feet deep

And if I am to endure that long-term sleep

Before I could tell you what you meant to me

A woman far better than the fraudulent that roam

Swallowing the earth whole spitting out broken bones

Bleeding hearts dry in this deserted land

How can I survive? Where do I belong? What do you
recommend?

The deceitful lies I'm told on the day to day basis

Crooked smile behind friendly faces

Who am I to trust

The world is becoming dust

When the only satisfaction is lust

Whatever happened to the women that made you smile?

Whatever happened to the women that made you happy?

Whatever happened to the women that had faith in you?

And would be by your side when you were down and out

Whatever happened to the women who were fearless?

Fear Less is something these women don't understand today

But there is one woman I can honestly say that is all these things

Skylight

She can tame the beast inside of me with a whisper

Be as addicting as my favorite liquor

Be a force to reckon with like the cosmic wind

She always has my back there's no need to pretend

Never fake, dumb or numb to the senses of my consensus

She is sensitive

Soft but not weak

Strong but still sweet

She is the only the woman that can make a man out of me

Raushan Mahdee

Falling

Diving through the atmosphere

With no fears

Earth's surface approaching fast

Thinking about my past

And I don't care

About anyone that came before you

The moment I looked into your eyes

I knew it was true

My stone-cold heart is warm

The perfectly imperfect

Soul of the world

Distilled such specific a form

For me to adore

I feel like I'm finally at peace

No longer at war

Lack of communication left me with battle scars

Sometimes I didn't know who I was fighting for

The only thing I know for sure

You are mine and I am yours

Skylight

The Sea

In the open sea

It's just you and me

Don't you see?

In my sights

Something bright

While we cruise

As we float

Like drift wood

The great blue

Puts me in

Uh

Good Mood

Resembling

Green eyes

Full lips

And thick thighs

Dark hair, crowned with

Purple tulips

Your presences force

The tides

World

Wide

Water grazing the sand

Eroding the turf

While I stand

Feeling the blistering surf

Course through my veins

Composure maintained

Thunder

Rolling

In

Dropping on

This

Terrain

As the clouds rain

Till they're drained

Your zephyr dissipates all of my pain

Shower me with your affection

The moon light dances in your reflection

Underneath the night sky

Skylight

Such ecstasy

Gave me the feeling to fly

Photographs

And dark rooms

To consume

From afar

Oh, queen of dreams can I swim in your sea of stars?

Catching memories inside a jar

Stay ajar

To the opp-per-tu-na-dees of

Internal feelings

Lasting for an e-tur-na-tee

Don't you see?

From beginning to end, it comes down to

Just you and me

Raushan Mahdee

-Shattered

Skylight

<u>07</u> May 2017

"Sometimes great things come from patiently waiting."

Raushan Mahdee

Son and Daughter

Sons and daughters

Mothers and fathers

Don't delete the feeling of love

For likes and followers

The internet has ruined

Our communication with one another

We have tons of ways to keep in contact

But I still don't talk to my brothers

It bothers me to know that

It's a fact or a notion of being ignored

Slept on

Kept unnoticed by the world

What on earth am I doing here if I can't get along with my blood

Flooded with information

I know it's dense

Finding solutions on cable or maybe a situation

On your favorite sitcom

Relax

Stay calm

Skylight

No need to be tense

Common sense is a gift

But senseless violence is used to uplift

A gathering of misfits

Mishaps have misshapen

Our worth

Self-preserved but also disturbed

Quiet living in the suburbs

Interrupted by the media

We're enclosed in a cage by our own fears

Can't differentiate the similarities between rain drops and tears

Gotta be passionate, don't be a pacifist

Gotta fight for your right to give a shit

Stand up and don't quit

The future is dim, but you're the brightest part of it

Son or Daughter

This is your father

Strive for longevity

With your kre-ate-tiv-a-tee

And I guarantee you it will take you further

Raushan Mahdee

Don't let the temptations of this world

Hold you back

Let God hold your hand

And keep your life on track

Or whatever you may believe in

That's your decision

Use that undying fire in your heart

To start something that cannot be

Easily extinguished

Be better than me

Become distinguished

Become someone great

Don't wait too late

Don't make the same mistakes as I did

When you're at a bar writing a poem for your unborn kids

"It's all about knowing the great unknown. When you're encapsulated inside a tiny box. That's where ignorance grows and you begin to ignore the world around you; instead of exploring outside your little comfort zone."

Raushan Mahdee

<u>Skylight Part Three</u>

Lying down and looking up

The family was looking down to see what's up

One said, "I knew he wouldn't amount to much"

Another said, "Yeah, I knew that boy was touched"

Soft padded satin surrounds the dearly departed

That long-term sleep that he long awaited

Turns out it was instigated

Skylight

Nobody should be afraid of the way they appear

Buried and besieged by fear

Hate has caused a hell of a coincidence

And manifested a series of unfortunate events

Balance is the key to be free of ignorance

Can't have the wrong without the right

Clouds rolling in sight

We need to find a middle ground for us to unite

So that dark stormy nights can bring forth daybreak and
produce Skylight

Raushan Mahdee

Misery part 2

...never mind what hell I'm living in

I really should be thanking you

You guided me to the truth

No longer a youth

No longer a fool

Eyes uncovered from the sheep's wool

You brought me back to a clear understanding of perception

Never

The

Less

It was tough to see pass reflections

Of my own past life's sacrifice

I got the die in my hand and I'm willing to roll the dice

I got dark thoughts inside of my skull

Scraping against

The surface of my mind, body and soul

The search for self is everlasting

Now I'm ready for the task at hand

No need to keep on asking

Some things will never change

Skylight

World views still deranged

This place is very strange

O Misery you're a mystery

And a curse throughout my history

I'm counting my blessings

Relearning my lessons

Coming into fruition

But what is life without its complications?

Misery made me feel hopeless

But there's no need to act reckless

Keeping my head up and going forward

No telling what I'm heading towards

Plans of action

Don't always lead towards satisfaction

Can't live with remorse

Too early to be a corpse

Gotta let God's Will run its course

-Evolution

www.ingramcontent.com/pod-product-compliance
Lightning Source LLC
Chambersburg PA
CBHW071937020426
42331CB00010B/2912